A Look at Space

The Moon

by Rebecca Sabelko

BLASTOFF! BEGINNERS,
AN IMPRINT OF
BELLWETHER MEDIA
BY FLUTTERBEE

Blastoff! Beginners are developed by literacy experts and educators to meet the needs of early readers. These engaging informational texts support young children as they begin reading about their world. Through simple language and high frequency words paired with crisp, colorful photos, Blastoff! Beginners launch young readers into the universe of independent reading.

Sight Words in This Book

about	is	made	on	to
big	it	make	the	
can	look	of	they	

This edition first published in 2027 by Bellwether Media, Inc.

Library of Congress Cataloging-in-Publication Data

Names: Sabelko, Rebecca author
Title: The moon / by Rebecca Sabelko.
Description: Minneapolis, Minnesota : Bellwether Media, Inc, 2027. | Series: A look at space | Includes bibliographical references and index. | Audience: Ages 4-7 | Audience: Grades K-1 | Summary: "Developed by literacy experts and educators for students in PreK through grade two, this book introduces beginning readers to the moon through simple, predictable text and related photos"-- Provided by publisher.
Identifiers: LCCN 2026011463 (print) | LCCN 2026011464 (ebook) | ISBN 9798893049060 library binding | ISBN 9798898802769 paperback | ISBN 9798898801335 ebook Subjects: LCSH: Moon
Classification: LCC QB582 .S23 2026 (print) | LCC QB582 (ebook)
LC record available at https://lccn.loc.gov/2026011463
LC ebook record available at https://lccn.loc.gov/2026011464

ISBN: 9798893049060 (hardcover)
ISBN: 9798898802769 (paperback)
ISBN: 9798898801335 (ebook)

Editor: Suzane Nguyen   Designer: Laura Sowers

Printed in the United States of America, North Mankato, MN.

Table of Contents

A Bright Moon!

The moon is
full tonight.
It is bright!

The moon is made of rock. It is round.

The moon moves around Earth.

It takes
about 27 days
to circle Earth.

KeyAren

Earth pulls
the moon.
They stay
close together.

the moon

Space rocks can hit the moon. They make **craters**.

craters

Tiny bits
of broken rocks
make **moondust**.

moondust

Sunlight shines on the moon. The moon **reflects** the light.

Phases make the moon look different every night!

About the Moon

The Moon

Things the Moon Has

craters

moondust

phases

Glossary

holes on the surface of an object

tiny, dry pieces of the moon

the stages of the moon that change the moon's shape

throws back light

To Learn More

ON THE WEB

FACTSURFER

Factsurfer.com gives you a safe, fun way to find more information.

1. Go to www.factsurfer.com.
2. Enter "the moon" into the search box and click 🔍.
3. Select your book cover to see a list of related content.

Index

The images in this book are reproduced through the courtesy of: wasan, front cover; ismailbasdas, pp. 3, 22 (moon); astrosystem, pp. 4-5, 8-9; Shukri, pp. 6-7; NASA Goddard Space Flight Center Image by Reto Stöckl/ Wikipedia, pp. 8, 22 (Earth); Dene' Miles, pp. 10-11; NASA/ Bill Anders/ Wikipedia, pp. 12-13; simon, pp. 14-15; NASA/ Wikipedia, pp. 16-17; Daniele, pp. 18-19; AGUS, pp. 20-21; Magere Hein/ Wikipedia, p. 22 (craters); Rawpixel.com, p. 22 (moondust); Delphotostock, p. 22 (phases); dietwalther, p. 22 (craters); NASA/ Buzz Aldrin/ Wikipedia, p. 23 (moondust); Martin Gruber, p. 23 (phases); kc85, p. 23 (reflects).